LIGHTNING
BOLT
BOOKS™

Look Inside a Drone

How It Works

Brianna Kaiser

Lerner Publications • Minneapolis

Lerner Publications Company
An imprint of Lerner Publishing Group, Inc.
241 First Avenue North
Minneapolis, MN 55401 USA

For reading levels and more information, look up this title at www.lernerbooks.com.

Main body text set in Billy Infant Regular. Typeface provided by SparkType.

Photo Editor: Nicole Berglund

Library of Congress Cataloging-in-Publication Data

Names: Kaiser, Brianna, 1996- author.
Title: Look inside a drone : how it works / Brianna Kaiser.
Description: Minneapolis : Lerner Publications, [2024] | Series: Lightning bolt books. Under the hood | Includes bibliographical references and index. | Audience: Ages 6-9 | Audience: Grades 2-3 | Summary: "From filming movies to helping find people in danger, drones do it all. Discover important parts of drones and how these pieces work together so drones can fly"— Provided by publisher.
Identifiers: LCCN 2023011259 (print) | LCCN 2023011260 (ebook) | ISBN 9798765608364 (lib. bdg.) | ISBN 9798765624388 (pbk.) | ISBN 9798765615706 (epub)
Subjects: LCSH: Drone aircraft—Juvenile literature. | BISAC: JUVENILE NONFICTION / Transportation / General
Classification: LCC TL685.35 .K35 2024 (print) | LCC TL685.35 (ebook) | DDC 629.133/39—dc23/eng/20230330

LC record available at https://lccn.loc.gov/2023011259
LC ebook record available at https://lccn.loc.gov/2023011260

Manufactured in the United States of America
1-1009481-51490-5/19/2023

Table of Contents

All about Drones

A movie crew is filming from up high. But how is the crew filming? They use a drone!

Drones are aircraft without pilots or crew on board. Some drones are remote-controlled.

A person on the ground uses a remote to move the drone.

People are working to improve drones to fly and land on their own. These drones would use a special sensor.

Special sensors could make it so drones can move on their own.

Drones can do many things including making deliveries.

Drones can fly high and fast and make quick turns. They can reach places and people that larger aircraft cannot.

On the Job

Search and rescue teams fly drones to find people after natural disasters. The drones find safe paths for rescuers to save the people.

Drones can also deliver food and water. They get supplies to people before rescuers arrive. Then rescuers can focus on saving people.

A firefighter using a drone

A drone flying by a storm

Scientists use drones to map land and study weather and climate change. Drones can spot nearby storms and warn people of dangerous weather.

The military uses drones with cameras to watch what is happening on the ground. The drones can find people who need help or go into areas that are unsafe for soldiers.

Soldiers can look on a laptop to see what a drone found.

Flying High

Drones have sensors. They respond to a remote control. People use the remote control to move the drone to where they want it to go.

A drone's propeller

Motors spin a drone's propellers. The propellers lift drones up and down. They change speeds to move the drone in different directions.

To move forward, the front propellers slow down. **The rear propellers speed up. To turn left, the left propellers slow down. The right propellers speed up.**

Propellers help a drone move.

The drone's four propellers help it stay balanced when it flies.

Drones can have from one to eight propellers. Most have four propellers. These drones have an X or H shape.

Cool Parts

Drones come in all shapes and sizes. They can do many cool or helpful things. Some drones have special equipment.

Some drones are built with arms and claws. These help them move or lift heavy objects.

This drone has two arms with claws.

Some drones have special cameras. Thermal cameras can check buildings, temperatures, and more.

Some drones have night vision cameras to see in the dark.

Drones could be even more popular in the future.

Technology is always improving. Drones will get better and better. Keep an eye out for future drones!

Drone Diagram

propellers

motors

camera

Propellers in Depth

If a drone has one or two propellers, it uses less energy than a drone with more propellers. Then it can stay in the air longer. But these drones are not as stable as drones with more propellers. Making sharp turns and flying at fast speeds is challenging. A drone with more propellers is more stable.

Glossary

aircraft: any machine that can fly

climate: the usual weather conditions of a place

direction: the course or path in which something is moving

motor: a part of a drone that makes the propellers spin

natural disaster: a natural event such as a flood that causes damage

propeller: a part of a drone made of blades that makes the drone fly

sensor: a device that responds to changes in the environment

thermal: relating to heat

Learn More

Bolte, Mari. *Drones in Action*. Minneapolis: Lerner Publications, 2024.

Britannica Kids: Drones
https://kids.britannica.com/kids/assembly/view/214255

Clasky, Leonard. *Robots in the Sky*. New York: Cavendish Square, 2022.

Kiddle: Unmanned Aerial Vehicle Facts for Kids
https://kids.kiddle.co/Unmanned_aerial_vehicle

Linde, Barbara Martina. *Drones in the Water*. New York: PowerKids, 2020.

Time for Kids: Drones in Space
https://www.timeforkids.com/g34/drones-in-space/?rl=en-700

Index

Photo Acknowledgments

Image credits: TierneyMJ/Shutterstock, p. 4; Buena Vista Images/Getty Images, p. 5; Pakhnyushchyy/Getty Images, p. 6; boonchai wedmakawand/Getty Images, p. 7; Ashley Cooper/Getty Images, p. 8; Mike Chapman/Shutterstock, p. 9; kckate16/Shutterstock, p. 10; EvgeniyShkolenko/Getty Images, p. 11; Vasyliuk/Shutterstock, p. 12; Westend61/Getty Images, p. 13; Paul Souders/Getty Images, p. 14; Malorny/Getty Images, p. 15; Innocenti/Getty Images, p. 16; LademannMedia/Alamy, p. 17; mailfor/Getty Images, p. 18; Kite_rin/Shutterstock, p. 19; Den Rozhnovsky/Shutterstock, p. 20.

Cover: LALS STOCK/Shutterstock.